Skate

The wonderful world of
ice skating in prose,
poetry and pictures

Edited by Meredith Collins
Foreword by Jayne Torvill

Articles by Jackie Keily and
Hazel Forsyth, Curators at the
Museum of London.

Poems by Addison, Goethe,
McCullough, Wordsworth
and many more .

Skate
© All contributors and Pighog Press 2012

A CIP record for this publication is available from the British Library.

Design by curiouslondon.com

ISBN 978-1-906309-79-4

First published November 2012 by

Pighog Press

PO Box 145
Brighton BN1 6YU
England UK

info@pighog.co.uk
www.pighog.co.uk

Contents

An Introduction to Ice Skating

Jayne Torvill

I was introduced to ice skating at the age of eight, during a school trip to the Nottingham Ice Stadium. That experience lead me to fall in love with this beautiful and elegant sport, launching my dream career.

Chris and I have been so grateful for the opportunities our careers have granted us since winning a gold medal in 1984 with our Bolero routine. It has taken so much to get here, but we have had tremendous fun on the ice.

Choreographing and working with professional as well as new skaters is amazingly rewarding. Some of my favourite moments on the ice have to do with beginners finding an unknown passion for figure skating. Witnessing that transformation is wonderful.

I am thrilled that I can continue to be creative on the ice and encourage amateur skaters to embrace the ice and see where it takes them.

If it is your first time skating or your fiftieth, I encourage you to get your skates on!

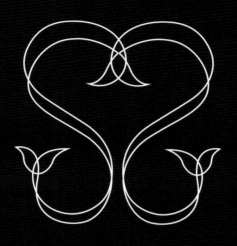

Essays

'A Brief History',
followed by essays from
Jackie Keily and Hazel
Forsyth, Curators at the
Museum of London

A Brief History of Ice Skating

Meredith Collins

Skating on ice as a means of transportation is mentioned in Scandinavian literature as early as 200 CE. However, the discovery of ice skates made from animal bones in Germany, Sweden, Switzerland and England suggests ice skating could date back 2000 years. And there's further archeological evidence for skate-like artifacts as long as 4000 years ago.

Bone skates were first used in Northern Europe and England. Made from the metacarpal bones of horses, deer, oxen and sheep, these skates were attached around the foot and ankle with thin leather straps. Because the bones were slippery, they made it difficult to dig into the ice for momentum. Often, in order to grip on icy surfaces when wearing these bone skates, long sticks were used for propulsion much like a modern punting pole.

Gradually the shape of the glider was improved to allow a more successful push-off from the ice. It wasn't until the 13th or 14th centuries that advancement in the design of these 'gliders' took place by the Dutch, who carved their skates into a more distinctive shape to aid momentum and control on the ice. The innovation of the Dutch ice skate most likely lead to the development of the first metal bladed skates that were introduced to Britain in the 14th century.

In 1498, an image of the Patron Saint of Skating Liedwi was printed, depicting the sixteen-year-old after being knocked down

Sonja Henie and partner compete in an ice-skating competition.
National Archives of Norway

on the ice, breaking her rib (below). Perhaps not a particularly beautiful print, as it focuses on her wincing face, it is the first pictorial record of an iron bladed ice skate – and the discomfort many learners feel when they fall over on the ice! Not only does this show the new apparatus being used for skating, but have a look at the man striding towards her in the background. He is skating in a modern fashion with his legs pushing himself across the ice. This movement indicates a more modern edged blade allowing him to skate in a technique that would not have been achievable with a bone skate.

Fig 1. This print was the first of its kind and was originally printed in the book 'Vita Alme Lydwine', written in 1498 by father Jan Brugman.

In William Fitz Stephen's account of Londoners skating on ice in the late 1100s, it is evident that sport and competition played a key role in gliding across the ice. This practice of competition developed into a performance of skill and would later establish the sport of speed skating. Skating was no longer a fumbling activity, but a practice of deliberate elegance and grace – despite the difficulty for women of skating in an abundance of petticoats. During the mid fifteenth century the Princess of Orange made an invaluable contribution to the evolution of skating by raising her skirts and tucking all of her draping layers into her waist. Although it meant her ankles were scandalously exposed, it gave her more mobility on the ice, as the cumbersome attire of the era was terribly constrictive. In shortening her skirts, the Princess of Orange risked being considered risqué, but it allowed women to enhance their performance on the ice.

Fig 2. A catalogue of shoes and boots printed in 1667 showed this drawing depicting a platform in a fiddle-shape with a runner blade that extended beyond the glider, curling upwards.

During the Great Frost of 1683 a great fair was constructed on the frozen River Thames. King Charles II and Queen Catherine arrived on the ice in a sledge drawn by an ice skater, many guests along the river, including diarist Samuel Pepys, joined them.

-

" The Dutch that in great
  Large shoals used to meet,
  And clap their crook'd scates on their foot,
  Now no more dare appear
  To make folken stare
  While on the smooth surface they float."
  (Dutch Ballad)

-

During this constant freeze, Pepys recorded the instantly favoured pastime of ice skating, which proved to be a fascinating outdoor recreation through the hard winter. He was an avid skater and wrote about various scenes that took place on the ice during the Great Frost Fairs. In the winter of 1662, Pepys wrote, "...over to the Parke (where I first in my life, it being great frost, did see people sliding with their skeats which is a very pretty art)...". Before then, skating had not been viewed as an art and would prove to flourish as a beautifully graceful sport.

In 1742 the Edinburgh Ice Skating Club was founded and was the first ice skating club in the world. In order to enter the club in the early part of the nineteenth century, one had to skate a complete circle on either foot and "it was also necessary to jump over first one, two and then three hats that were placed on the ice."[1] The formation of the Edinburgh Ice Skating Club was a fundamental part in the development of ice skating as an activity. During this time long distance skates needed to adapt to allow for more swift and precise figures being sketched into the ice. A variety of prototypes were experimented with to achieve a better shape for ease and agility. Many designs changed the traditional flat surface of a skate blade into a more curved blade as the flatter blades limited how skaters could move on the ice. These taller, thinner and more rounded blades would give the skater better mobility on the ice and the performance of various 'figures' could be carved into the ice with greater precision. (Fig 5. pp19)

---

[1]Brown, Nigel. Ice-Skating: A History (London, England: Nicholas Kaye Ltd, 1959), 39.

In the early skating of these figures, participants understood that this activity must be the development of an art. It was decided that not only should the finished figure carved into the ice appear beautiful and symmetric but it must also be gracefully achieved without lurching movements and flailing arms. However, skating backwards was still viewed as an unnecessary and horrendous practice. *(Fig 3. pp15)*

By 1795 the designs were becoming increasingly intricate and were practiced with such grace that a poetry in motion was acknowledged by famous poets of the era. Joseph Addison as well as Friedrich Gottlieb Klopstock wrote of the stunning displays they saw take place on the ice. And whilst many poets regarded ice skating from afar, Johann Wolfgang von Goethe practiced skating long into the night, letting his poetic imagination carve intricate patterns into the moonlit ice *(Opposite)*.

The cold winters of the 1820s brought about a new phenomenon of ice skating in the Fens of Cambridgeshire. By flooding the meadows of the Fens, the conditions for speed skating competitions were perfect. As an activity, skating became a spectator sport, where thousands of fans lined the ice to watch legendary ice skaters compete for cash prizes. Fenmen, Turkey Smart, Gutta Percha See and Larman Register were among the many speed skaters that made a name for themselves and went on to win international competitions and championships.

In the later half of the eighteenth century, the development of ice skating had virtually arrived at a standstill in England, while France saw a rise in the popularity of the activity based on the acceptance of skating in the court of Louis XVI. His interest made what the Parisians called 'sliding over ice' a fashionable activity, and because it was practiced by the noble and elite, 'sliding' was viewed as a highly graceful activity that required true poise. Instead of treating skating as an activity of grace and beauty, the English began to practice ice skating with an acute science to each movement, more like an athletic sport than the artful French 'sliding'.

The English worked technically, refining their repertoires of curves and turns, developing detailed combinations. Because Englishmen were concerned skating would be considered too

The Fool's Epilogue
Johann Wolfgang von Goethe

MANY good works I've done and ended,
Ye take the praise--I'm not offended;
For in the world, I've always thought
Each thing its true position hath sought.
When praised for foolish deeds am I,
I set off laughing heartily;
When blamed for doing something good,
I take it in an easy mood.
If some one stronger gives me hard blows,
That it's a jest, I feign to suppose:
But if 'tis one that's but my own like,
I know the way such folks to strike.
When Fortune smiles, I merry grow,
And sing in dulci jubilo;
When sinks her wheel, and tumbles me o'er,
I think 'tis sure to rise once more.

In the sunshine of summer I ne'er lament,
Because the winter it cannot prevent;
And when the white snow-flakes fall around,
I don my skates, and am off with a bound.
Though I dissemble as I will,
The sun for me will ne'er stand still;
The old and wonted course is run,
Until the whole of life is done;
Each day the servant like the lord,
In turns comes home, and goes abroad;
If proud or humble the line they take,
They all must eat, drink, sleep, and wake.
So nothing ever vexes me;
Act like the fool, and wise ye'll be!

effeminate if performed very gracefully, they focused more rigidly on the patterns that could be carved into the ice, and were unconcerned with how graceful their movements were. With this enhanced technical manner of practice, skating backwards became suddenly very necessary. *(Fig 4. Opposite)*

Many of the technically precise figures were given appropriately ostentatious names including: Jump of Zephyr, Courtesan and the Step of Apollo, which would all lead to the advancement of skating. Although performed stiffly by the English, the French made the movements much more beautiful and regarded the activity as a ballet-style dance. The technically perfect motions and the graceful conduct would all be incorporated to create what we consider figure skating today.

1830 saw the foundation of the Skating Club in London. As a member one had to wear the badge of the club, which was a miniature silver skate that hung from a ribbon tied to the member's buttonhole. This distinguished the club members from other skaters when practicing on ice rinks in London and was meant to inform onlookers that they were watching a true 'professional'. With the Skating Club came the development of 'combined skating'. But skating could not be enhanced without a more precise ice skate. In 1836 a Mr Henry Boswell of Oxford set about to develop a new, longer blade that allowed skaters the full ability to skate in more advanced figures forwards and backwards. This new ice skate greatly improved the precise and technically perfect figures that had become so fashionable in England during the nineteenth century.

Through its many forms and developments, perhaps the most revolutionary was the advancement of the skate designed in Philadelphia during the middle of the nineteenth century. The city had become an important skating centre and it was in Philadelphia around 1848 that the first all-metal skate was made. Invented by E.V. Buchness, the blade and base were to be made of iron and permanently attached to the boot, no longer strapped around the foot, which would allow for extra stability and control. This new invention spread the popularity of ice skating across America. Experiments on the design lead to improvements in advance of Europe's own ice skate design. American skaters were

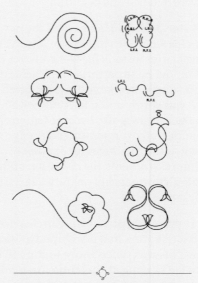

Fig 3. Figures etched into the ice.

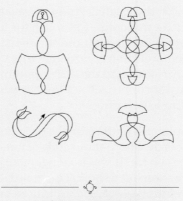

Fig 4. Intricate English figures

able to indulge in a quantity of intricate figures and completely new movements. By bringing gymnastic skills onto the ice the figures created were detailed and beautiful.

The American Skater, Jackson Haines used the new metal skates to perform his ambitious repertoire. Integrating ballet skills with skating figures he took his work all over Europe where he settled in Vienna to perform and teach. Creating his own ice skates, his solid and reliable design allowed a free-skating performance that was sturdy and safe. Along with his exceedingly detailed performance, Haines also became famous for his theatric displays and his amusing costumes (often dressing as a woman on the ice!) Known as the American Ice Skating King, he was admired for his impressive skills, his invention of the Sitspin as well as popularizing showmanship on the ice in a true 'dancing on ice' fashion.

While Jackson Haines was pirouetting on ice dressed as a woman, English ice skaters had developed a 'Victorian Stiff Style' of skating. This was much more technical than any other practice of ice skating at this time. Instead of focusing on the beautiful grace and artistry that was the main focus in Europe and America, the English style of ice skating featured careful precision in the execution of various figures, which were restrained and dignified. (Quite right too!) There was no frivolity expressed, and the top hats worn with black frock coats by the Skating Club members made rigidity unavoidable. While the Continent practiced ice skating with elegance and grace, the English stiffly conducted themselves across the ice with a masculine approach for fear of being regarded as effeminate. Though the enhanced and elaborate technicalities and precision regarded in this Victorian style was a terrific contribution to the development of skating, it was a terribly austere approach and music was very much removed from English skating.

In contrast, skating in Vienna (thanks to Jackson Heines) was becoming a spectacle where thousands of fans would go to see performances on ice. It was no longer considered just an exercise or recreation but a show. The theatrical displays and musical interpretation possessed unlimited possibilities for the development of skating as an art. The English continued to approach skating in a strict fashion, and were against developments that weren't in keeping with the combination-skating techniques they were perfecting.

The Victorian style in England offered women the opportunity to practice combination-skating through hand-in-hand skating designed for men and women. Named the Mercury Scud, this hand-in-hand figure allowed partners to skate together in the earliest form of pair skating. It relied on the harmonious movement of a couple rather than the perfection of a figure.

To develop skating in England, the creation of a union was encourage and in 1879 the foundation of the National Skating Association of Great Britain was formed for the promotion of speed-skating (enhancing its popularity in the Fens). The popularity of straight mile contests was phenomenal, and enthusiastic crowds gathered to witness championship races and cash prizes. While Victorian skaters were afraid their skating art might be transformed into a purely competition-driven activity, Denmark began the first 'artistic skating competitions'. Soon various categories were beginning to emerge in ice skating, and competitive skating was officially born at the first international competition in Vienna in 1882. The concept of carving figures into the ice as a form of art was slowly dropping out of fashion, and free-skating was introduced as a new category in performance on ice. Even outfits for ice skating were becoming smaller and more decorative, with fur collars and shorter skirts for women, making the activity aesthetically aware.

In London, in 1876. Mr John Gamgee built a small ice floor in the back room of his house in Chelsea. His patented refrigeration technique was used in the first artificial ice rink ever built, The London Glaciarium. It was a private rink, where only noblemen and gentlemen could be members, and where, finally, an orchestra accompanied English skaters. However, even with the new developments in skating, Britain was still very much practicing a stiffened skate and when Germany organised the first European Figure Skating Championships in 1891, England did not compete. Their style consisted of four skaters looping around an orange placed on the ice and it just wasn't good enough!

Europe was becoming more graceful on the ice. In 1894 the first official performance of the waltz on ice occurred in Paris. A year later, stiffly skating their way back to England, instructors brought proper ballroom dancing to the English. The 'ice-waltz' paired skating and dancing together in a graceful and technically challenging activity that would create what we now consider modern figure skating. The introduction of lifts and shadow skating became coupled with the ideas of Victorian hand-in-hand skating.

Finally the English were skating elegantly and with harsh competition. Dancing on ice became increasingly popular in the 1930s with every ice skater aspiring to perform the waltz on ice alongside the tango and ten-step. With the Norwegian skating protégé, Sonja Henie returning to Hollywood, skating not only became a fancy exhibition of skill and style but it was now the key to show business.

Since the twentieth century, the English style of precision and technique has remained an artful skill of remarkable competition and has influenced nations and skaters the world over. Modern Olympic figure skating has developed from hand-in-hand skating and speed skating to become what we recognize as competitive skating today. British ice skating legends such as Jayne Torvill and Christopher Dean have further redefined the style and grace of skating performance and dancing on ice. With each performance, skaters today demonstrate the evolution of ice skating over centuries, not to mention a bit of added glitter!

Further Reading
Bert van Voorbergen. The Virtual Ice Skates Museum. 2 February 2002. Web. October 2012.

Brown, Nigel. Ice-Skating: A History. London: Nicholas Kaye Ltd., 1959. Print.

Slater, J. Fen Speed Skating: An Illustrated History. March, 2000. Print.

Syers, Edgar Wood. The Poetry of Skating. London: Watts & Co., 1905. Print.

Fig 5. Revd Dr Robert Walker Skating on Duddingston Loch
by Sir Henry Raeburn Scottish National Gallery

The Coldest Winter on Record

17th Century Frost Fairs
Hazel Forsyth, Museum of London Curator

The great 'singularity of the City of London' is the Thames, wrote
James Dalton in his celebratory account of the capital in 1580, for it,

> "*Reacheth furthest in the bellie of the land [and]... the breadth and
> stilnesses of the water is naviagable up and down the streame.'
> London is perfectly situated 'for if it were removed more to the
> west, it should lose the benefit of the ebbing and flowing; and
> if it were seated more towardes the East, it should be nearer to
> daunger of the enemie and further from the good ayre and from
> doing good to the inner parts of the Realme.*"

The importance of the river to the communication, economy
and culture of the capital is a recurring theme in sixteenth and
seventeenth-century literature. Foreigners were particularly struck
by the vast number of merchant vessels thronging the quays and
wharves and the smaller craft 'used by groups of people to cross
the river, or to enjoy themselves in the evenings'. According to the
Venetian, Alesandro Magno in 1562, the boats were 'charmingly
upholstered and embroidered cushions are laid across the seats,
which are very comfortable to sit on or lean against'. By the late 16th
century there were three-thousand watermen operating a water-
taxi service on the Thames, but sometimes there were no boats to
be had and one tourist complained that he had waited so long 'that
we could in the space of time have made the entire journey on foot
and performed some errands along the way'. When the boat finally
arrived it appeared to be reduced by 'worms and time to such a

The Frozen Thames, looking Eastwards towards Old London Bridge 1677
by Abraham Hondius © Museum of London

condition that it could have been used as a cork' and the two watermen seemed broken: 'they stretched their bodies to their entire lengths while rowing, [they] succeeded only in making very slow progress.'

The general hustle and bustle of the river came to an abrupt stop in winters of prolonged and severe cold. The Thames froze and the ice was so thick that Londoners spilled on to its surface for games and amusements. In 1564, Elizabeth I 'went on the ice daily' for archery practice and in the winter of 1607/8 the citizens took 'tumultuous possession' with dancing, bowls, and 'variable pastimes, by reason of which sellers, vituallers, that sold beere and wine etc' set up boothes on the ice. There were booths on the frozen Thames in the winter of 1621, and a lake of ice formed on the marshy-ground to the north of the City in Moorfields and Shoreditch, where London apprentices made great slides and constructed toboggans from blocks of ice. Skates were fashioned from the 'leg-bones of some animal, under the soles of their feet' and the skaters propelled themselves along with an iron-spiked staff so that they moved with the 'velocity of a flight of a bird, or a bolt discharged from a cross-bow'. Accidents were not uncommon. *(Opposite)*

The Thames froze on twelve occasions in the course of the 17th century and in the frost of 1662, Londoners began to use iron-bladed skates from Holland. The coldest winter on record was in 1683/4 when the freeze lasted from the beginning of December until the 4 February. Men and animals perished, trees split assunder and as the diarist John Evelyn put it, 'London, by reason of the excessive coldnesse of the aire, hindring the ascent of the smoke, was so filled with the fuliginous steam of the Sea-Coale, that hardly could one see crosse the street'. The fog was so dense that people struggled to breathe; water pipes froze solid 'with disastrous accidents', and the Thames froze to a great depth, supporting 'a Citty or Continual faire...a bacchanalia, Triumph or Caroval on the Water.' Londoners tottered on to the ice in their droves and contemporary paintings show a double-line of tented boothes stretching across the river from Temple Stairs to the Old King's Barge-House. One enterprising printer set up shop on the ice, charging customers six-pence for a personalized souvenir and kiosks sold all sorts of commodities, hot drinks, roasted-meats, snacks and trinkets. There were fox hunts, puppet-shows and carriage races and some of the passenger boats were set on wheels and rigged with sails so that they could glide across the ice.

A Frost Fair on the Thames at Temple Stairs 1684
by Abraham Hondius © Museum of London

Ice skating:
the bare bones

Jackie Keily, Museum of London Curator

People have long found the grace and speed of ice skating to be
an entertaining pastime. Today, professional and amateur skaters
alike enjoy the sport with the help of ice skating boots, complete
with metal blades that glide through the ice. However, ice skating
predates the modern boot. So how did skating enthusiasts in
medieval London propel themselves across the ice? They
wore animal bones tied to their feet of course. We are lucky
enough at the Museum of London to have both some of the
bone ice skates themselves and also a written account of what
it was like to use them.

In the past it was not uncommon for the Thames to freeze over,
as well as other marshy areas of the capital, such as Moorfields to
the north of Moorgate in the City of London. A vivid description,
written by William Fitz Stephen in the late 1100s, tells how
London youths played on the ice at Moorfields:

> " When the great marsh that washes the Northern walls of
> the City is frozen, dense throngs of youths go forth to disport
> themselves upon the ice.' Some people skidded and slid on
> their feet, whilst others were pulled around by their friends on
> ice seats. But the most skilled were the ice-skaters: 'who fit to
> their feet the shin-bones of beasts, lashing them beneath their
> ankles, and with iron-shod poles in their hands they strike
> ever and anon against the ice."

Fig 6. Bone Ice skate
12th Century © Museum of London

Although this sounds like madness to us, it did indeed work and we have the proof in the many bone ice skates that have been recovered from archaeological excavations in London and elsewhere. It appears that in most cases the skates were attached to the foot with a leather thong, and the skater pushed themselves along using one or two wooden poles tipped with an iron spike. These skates were cheap and easy to make. The bones most commonly used are the lower limb bones (metapodials and radii) from horses and cattle, although occasionally deer and other animal bones were used. *(Fig 6. pp25)*

Very little re-working of the bone was required. Usually, a hole was drilled at one end – the heel end - into which a wooden peg or nail could be fitted to attach a leather thong or cord. A small number of skates have been found with their wooden pegs still in situ. At the other end – the toe end - a little working was done to make it more pointed and sometimes a horizontal hole was drilled for the leather thong to be laced through.

Some skates have slightly upswept toes and this would have helped where there was light snow on the ground. What would become the base was roughly smoothed to allow it to be balanced on. Once the skates were attached to your feet, and you had a pole or perhaps a pair to cling onto, you were ready to go, and go people did! To quote again from Fitz Stephen, '(they) are borne along swift as a bird in flight or a bolt shot from a mangonel' (a mangonel is a medieval siege engine or catapult).

The Swede Olaus Magnus, writing in the 1500s, described how some skaters greased their bone skates with pork fat so that they would move more easily on the ice. Many of the skates that are found archaeologically show signs of use, including wear marks on the base of the bones. Some bone skates lack any attachment holes but still show signs of wear and use. In these instances the skater must have balanced on the skates and used the poles to propel themselves forward, no easy feat to undertake.

The earliest bone skates are found in Eastern Europe, dating to the second millennium BC. A small number have been found in Britain and elsewhere in Europe from late Iron Age and Roman times, but they are more commonly found from the Viking and Anglo-Saxon periods, from the 8th to 9th centuries AD onwards.

Archaeological evidence suggests that bone skates were used throughout the medieval period. However, once metal-bladed skates became common, the rather more cumbersome bone skates were largely abandoned. But metal-bladed skates are not commonly found in Britain until the late 17th century and in rural parts of northern and Eastern Europe bone skates continued in use into the early 20th century. It is likely that bone skates continued as a cheap and easily made alternative, although perhaps one whose technique took a bit longer to perfect.

A number of modern researchers and historical re-enactors have tried out skating on bone skates. All of them have found that the skates work but that it took considerable time to work out the best way to attach the skates and the best method of propelling oneself along the ice. The consensus, however, is that with practice a good speed can be achieved. As with modern skating there was the potential for this to be a dangerous as well as a fun sport. Modern experiments have concluded that, perhaps unsurprisingly, the injuries caused by skating on bone skates are similar to those when skating on modern metal-bladed skates. Indeed, William Fitz Stephen describes quite graphically what could happen in the 12th century:

> *" But sometimes two by agreement run one against the other from a great distance and, raising their poles, strike one another. One or both fall, not without bodily hurt, since on falling they are borne a long way in opposite directions by the force of their own motion; and wherever the ice touches the head, it scrapes and skins it entirely. Often he that falls breaks shin or arm, if he fall upon it."*

However, I'm sure, as with today's skaters, the fun outweighed the risk of injury. So next time you go out on the ice spare a thought for your medieval London predecessors and enjoy the ease with which your blades slice the ice.

Further Reading

Hans Chrisitan Küchelmann and Petar Zidarov, 2005, 'Let's skate together! Skating on bones in the past and today', in 'From hooves to horns, from mollusc to mammoth: manufacture and use of bone artefacts from Prehistoric times to the present', edited by H. Luik, A. M. Choyke, C. E. Batey and L. Lõugas, Talinn

Arthur MacGregor, 1976, 'Bone skates: a review of the evidence', Archaeological Journal, 133 (1976), 57-74

Arthur MacGregor, 1985, 'Bone, antler, ivory and horn: the technology of skeletal materials since the Roman period', Croom Helm, Bechenham

William Fitz Stephen, 1990, 'Norman London', Italica Press, New York

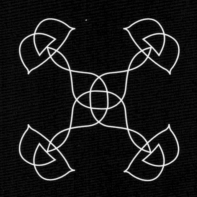

Poems

by Addison, Goethe, McCullough, Wordsworth and many more

No Torvill and Dean
Tracy Davidson

I'm no Torvill and you're no Dean,
wobbling our way around the rink.
We seem to lack the skating gene.
I'm no Torvill and you're no Dean.
With all the grace of Mr Bean
we stagger like we're on the drink.
I'm no Torvill and you're no Dean,
wobbling our way around the rink.

An Elfin Skate
Eugene Lee-Hamilton, 1892

They wheeled me up the snow-cleared garden way,
And left me where the dazzling heaps were thrown;
And, as I mused on winter sports once known,
Up came a tiny man to where I lay.
He was six inches high; his beard was grey
As silver frost; his coat and cap were brown,
Of mouse's fur; while two wee skates hung down
From his wee belt, and gleamed in winter's ray.
He clambered up my couch, and eyed me long.
"Show me thy skates," said I; " for once, alas,
I too could skate. What pixie mayst thou be?"
"I am the king, " he answered, "of the throng
Called Winter Elves. We dwell 'neath roots, and pass
The summer months in sleep. Frost sets us free.

"We find by moonlight little pools of ice,
Just one yard wide," the imp of winter said;
"And skate all night, while mortals are in bed,
In tiny circles of our Elf device;
And when it snows we harness forest mice
To wee bark sleighs with lightest fibrous thread,
And scour the woods; or play all night instead
With snow balls large as peas, well patted thrice.
But is it true, as I have heard them say,
That thou can'st share in winter games no more,
But liest motionless year in, year out?
That must be hard. To-day I cannot stay,
But I'll return each year, when all is hoar,
And tell thee when the skaters are about."

On my wheeled bed I let my fingers play
With a wee silver skate, scarce one inch long,
Which might have fitted one of Frost's Elf throng,
Or been his gift to one whose limbs are clay.
But Elfdom's dead; and what in my hand lay
Was out of an old desk; from years when, strong
And full of health, life sang me still its song;
A skating club's small badge, long stowed away.
Oh, there is nothing like the skater's art-
The poetry of circles; nothing like
The fleeting beauty of his crystal floor.
Above his head, the winter sunbeams dart;
Beneath his feet, flits fast the frightened pike.
Skate while you may; the morrow skates no more.

Skating
William Wordsworth, 1850

And in the frosty season, when the sun
Was set, and visible for many a mile
The cottage windows blazed through twilight gloom,
I heeded not their summons; happy time
It was indeed for all of us- for me
It was a time of rapture! Clear and loud
The village clock tolled six- I wheeled about,
Proud and exulting like an untried horse
That cares not for his home. All shod with steel,
We hissed along the polished ice in games
Confederate, imitative of the chase
And woodland pleasures- the resounding horn,
The pack loud chiming, and the hunted hare.
So through the darkness and the cold we flew,
And not a voice was idle; with the din
Smitten, the precipices rang aloud.
The leafless trees and every icy crag
Tinkled like iron; while far distant hills
Into the tumult sent an alien sound
Of melancholy not unnoticed, while the stars
Eastward were sparkling clear, and in the west
The orange sky of evening died away.
Not seldom from the uproar I retired
Into a silent bay, or sportively
Glanced sideways, leaving the tumultuous throng,
To cut across the reflex of a star
That fled, and, flying still before me, gleamed
Upon the glassy plain; and oftentimes,
When we had given our bodies to the wind,
And all the shadowy banks on either side
Came sweeping through the darkness, spinning still
The rapid line of motion, then at once
Have I, reclining upon my heels,
Stopped short; yet still the solitary cliffs
Wheeled by me- even as if the earth had rolled
With visible motion her diurnal round!

Scating: A Poem
Joseph Addison, 1720

See! Nature round a hoary Prospect yields,
And Beds of Snow conceal the whit'ned Fields;
Shoot their keen Dars, and, mingling, fill the Sky.
The silent Streams in Murmurs cease to move,
Lock'd in their Shores by Icy Bands above:
No more through Vales They draw their hard'ned Train,
But form, unmov'd, a silent Silver Plain.
The Watry Gods who dwell in Courts below
Lament their stubborn Waves no longer flow;
Each sad to view the Empire where he Reigns
Enclosed above, and bound with Chrystal Chains.

Yet this bleak Season of th' inclement Year
Can boast Delights the smiling Youth to cheer;
With vig'rous Sports the Winter Rage defy,
New-brace the Nerves, and active Life supply.

Each now the Labour hardy to endure,
Who boast a steddy Strength, and tread secure,
With panting Joy the frozen Kingdom gain,
Rush to the Shore, and hide the crackling Plain.
Now in long Tracts with failing Speed they shoot,
And tire unarm'd the Vigour of the Foot;
Now o'er the Race in winding Circles wheel,
Drove round, and carried on their shining Steel.

See! There the Youth with eager Passion glow,
Bound from above, and fill the Plains below.
Skim lightly o'er the Waves, and scarce deface
With beauteous Prints the Silver shining Race.
See! In the midst of their smooth Jouney, skilled,
They stop, and turn, and mark the flitt'ring Field.
Razing the Surface, on they wheel around,
Which bends and yields, and cracks beneath the Wound.
They o'er the Chase with easy Labour drove,
Now here, now there, in endless Mazes move.

If we such Pleasures from its Rigour gain,
The Winter sheds its keenest Rage in vain,
While with full Joy the beating Heart o'erflows,
And the fair Cheek with fairer Purple glows.
Here, if by chance unable to convey
Too great a Weight, the parting Ice give way,
Or the bright Knots which on its Surface rise
Oerturn the hasty Racer as he Flies,
What shouts, what Laughter, fill the Echoing Skies!
No Pity in one merry Face appears,
The Wretch o'erwhelm'd with Jokes instead of Tears;
This treacherous Feet and Garments, as they show,
Augment his Fellow's Joy, the Hero's Woe.

But if, descending on the slippery Plain,
The rival Youth for Fame and Glory strain,
Shoot from the barrier, and, with wishful Eye
To reach the Goal, bend forward as they fly;
Breathless, around their eager Arms they throw,
And lend new swiftness to their Feet below,
No even Tracks confess their winding Way,
Confus'd they cross, and in Meanders play
Orb within org, their sportive Toil we view,
Whit'ning with Steel, the Circles where they flew.
So when a Swallow wantons in the Air,
The Spring arriv'd, and smiling Season Fair,
In doubtful Mazes she her flight pursues,
Now sips the Stream, now drinks the fragrant dews;
Now skims the flow'ry Meadows, but to rise,
Anon more lofty, and regain her Skies.
Her airy windings each with Joy Surveys,
Views her quick Turns, and wonders as she plays.

Skilled in these Arts (if not by Fame bely'd)
When chilling Winters bind the solid Tide,
Their ancient Tracks the Belgian Realms disdain,
For nearer Paths along the frozen Main.
The sliding Traveller will now no more
Regard the Mazes of the winding Shore;
Pleas'd o'er the Waves, his Pleasures does pursue,
With longing Eyes some absent Friend to view,
Or gaze on distant Cities which arise
In foreign Realms, and warm'd by foreign Skies.

Now to the faithful Sea the Matron dares
Herself commit, and trust her brittle Wares;
Fearless the flying Dame, least she of they,
By chance o'erturn'd, should sink, the Ocean's Prey,
With shining Furrows all the Plain abounds
Her Ice Journey mark'd with Silver Wounds.

T.S Eliot Goes Dancing on Ice with Ruth Belville
(To the Worshipful Company of London Clockmakers)
Pauline Suett Barbieri

They meet at a 'Kiss and Cry' outside the Stock Exchange.
'Would you care to dance?' Eliot asks Ruth, taking her hand
whilst eyeing 'Arnold', her silver pocket chronometer.
'I see you have time, dear Ruth, time for the buyer, time for the seller,
time for the man who puts the wick in our tallow.'
Into the cold, thin, stillness of finance, the pair glide.

It doesn't matter what kind of salchow they do, or how
the scissors of justice push old thread through a new needle
because this 'Time Pirate' steers them towards
the Millennium Bridge and the twenty first century,
where a rusty Household gate lets in all manner of things.
A haircutter winds her watch away from the Serpentine
while Eliot creates a new axle-burning rose.

Over sixty years on, the Tower again rattles in chains
as City banks flutz a series of improperly executed flips.
The dancers skirt the frosty dome of St. Paul's, stumble
over pavement protesters housed along a technicoloured grapevine.
'But there is only time,' says Ruth. And the past yelps
like a steel dog caught in the jaws of London's gaping bridge.

Eliot chacks Ruth at the Temple, turns a new toe loop,
whispers to the money changers, 'There is only the dance.'
He blades the flickering lamps in Downing Street which emulates
the perpetual possibilities of the river and its mud.
Algae brackets cash as Ruth prices the clocks.
But the dance is never expected . The judges sail by,
as usual, on the golden barge of indecision.

A swizzle of fish silvers the wallets dangling under Westminster
Bridge. 'Every stag leap has to segue the rhythm of dance,' Eliot says,
while shooting a wild duck along the milky embankment.
'It appears there is only the making,' says Ruth.
With a heart all through with bleeding,
Eliot says, 'Or rather, only the undertaking.'

The pair melt slowly into a navy blue Thames
as a gazetteer of stars tells the time of London's own undoing.

'Ruth Belville'- also known as the 'Greenwich Time Lady' sold the time on the streets
of London from 1892-1930.
'Kiss and Cry'- that part of the outer rink where skaters wait for competition results.
'Time Pirates'- Victorian Londoners who looked over Ruth's shoulder.

The Midnight Skaters
Edmund Blunden

The hop-poles stand in cones,
The icy pond lurks under,
The pole-tops steeple to the thrones
Of stars, sound gulfs of wonder;
But not the tallest thee, 'tis said,
Could fathom to this pond's black bed.
Then is not death at watch
Within those secret waters?
What wants he but to catch
Earth's heedless sons and daughters?
With but a crystal parapet
Between, he has his engines set.

Then on, blood shouts, on, on,
Twirl, wheel and whip above him,
Dance on this ball-floor thin and wan,
Use him as though you love him;
Court him, elude him, reel and pass,
And let him hate you through the glass.

Skating
Robert Snow, 1845

When to his feet the skater binds his wings,
As of Jove's messenger the poet sings,
He, like the hare, outstrips the Northern wind,
And casts, in doubling, a keen glance behind.
By art that to the frozen lake conveys
A glowing interest in winter days,
Before the gazer now he seems to fly,
Now with a backward stroke deludes the eye;
Precipitating curves on curves anew,
Retuning ever, to his centre true.
With air of noble ease, and swan-like grace,
He balances awhile in narrow space;
Then sweeps far round with power not shown before,
And on his crystal plain does all but soar.
Yet is his pastime brief; the solar heat
Grows strong; again the lapsing waters meet,
And to dull, plodding earth confine his daring feet.

The Skaiter's March
C. Dibdin, Written for the Edinburgh Skating Club, 1802

This snell and frosty morning,
With rhind the trees adorning,
Tho' Phoebus below,
Through the sparkling snow,
A skaiting we go,
With a fal, lal, lal, lal, lal, lal,
To the sound of the merry, merry horn.

From the right to the left we're plying,
Swifter than winds we're flying,
Spheres with spheres surrounding,
Health and strength abounding.
In circles we sweep,
Our poise still we keep.
Behold how we sweep
The face of the deep,
With a fal, lal, lal, lal, lal,
To the sound of the merry, merry horn.

Great Jove looks down with wonder
To view his sons of thunder.
Tho' the water he sea,
We rove on our heel;
Our weapons are steel,
And no danger we feel,
With a fal, lal, lal, lal, lal,
To the sound of the merry, merry horn.

See! The Club advances,
See how they join the dances,
Horns and trumpets sounding,
Rocks and hills resounding.
Let Tritons now blow,
For Neptune below
His beard dares not shew,
Of call us his foe,
With a fal, lal, lal, lal, lal,
To the sound of the merry, merry horn.

Tolstoy on Ice
Anna Kisby

And if we should come upon them once again as we glide
a finger across a screen, find them spinning still on a rink
preserved in these woods, shall we see her as one sees the
sun without looking, and shall we fall in love all again with
the turn of her elastic little foot, with his peasant beard and
violent effort to impress

     and then what if her handkerchief blooms
upon the ice like an O'Keeffe flower, or if this time her muff
begs attention for it is splintered so with hoar-crystals
we may only read as warnings of marital strife
then might we take a pick-axe
to our brain

     and from its worming parts lifts squealing
between finger and thumb, a girl and a book.
Life, she thinks, will be Russia. Bless her.
Skim forward so the fine print blurs the boring bits
like snow in the eyes, a zoetrope
of faces, branches, sky

     passed, passed, passed. Forget
the train of events, the awful end.
Wink, and call her *tiny bear* before she slips
     again into the deep dark forest

Verses Ynne Praise of Scating
Edgar Wood Syers, 1904

Lett hym goe daunce yn rounds and rings
      Who n'eer effaied to scaite;
Whan shodde lyke Mercurie wyth wyngs,
      Wee envie no man's state.

Whan fast onne glaffie playne wee glyde
      Lyke martlets farre and free,
Fifhers who snare the finnie trybe
      Knowe no suche lybertie.

The curler's skyppe may ufe hym ille
      Wee envie not hys lotte,
E'een whan bye luckie chaunce or skylle
Hee hath putt downe "the shotte."

Whan blythe and gaye our scaiters are,
      Whythe edges firm and true,
The gouffer's joye ys leffe bye farr
      Shoulde hee hold outte yn two.

Crescendo
Curtis Tappenden

It started with a crescendo,
our Bolero!
me, in purple hood,
sleeves bagging in the chill night;
ice-packed floor alight with the warmth
of coloured spots and the elegant dance.
Inspired, we admired dancer blades carving the route
in a night city court,
closing our chapter on a tale of winter love,
complete.

And then you,
you entered fearless and falling into the barriers
with purity and accidental grace;
my clumsy mind wobbling blind as
plum leggings and silky trailing scarf
cast you as the perfect score.
At once in skater dreams,
our edge-running unison sparked and forged,
steel blades leapt into crystal spirals,
and double jumps tripled as heartbeats raged
and quickened.

And then it was us,
envisioned glassy love perfected in motion
near unstoppable- breaks sudden,
skates lock sharp, legs twist and splay and tumble;
a commotion and clatter of incompetent dreamers.
Drawn back from the sweeping magic
where the stars now dance and spin our heads,
they still aspire as champions kindling Bolero's fire
and a return tomorrow where I think
our passionate crescendo will loop the rink.

Love on Ice
Brendan Cleary

1

dizzy with love
unsteady on my feet

slippin' about a bit
or even more

but I'll hold you tight
& then we'll glide

2

we'll glide
& forget ourselves

who we were
it's not important

not on this ice

3

'slip slidin' away'
the song goes

look! that girl
over there!

she seems to know
how to do it

4

remember not standin' for the queen
at the ice rink at Whitley Bay
remember The Durham Wasps
remember your back so smooth
it was all to sudden for sure

5

walkin' past the iceworks
on North Shields pier
I must have been stupid

& now I'm wiser
& if you don't hang on to someone
then you'll fall, you'll fall

6

take the cycle gear off
& go for ice

I'll get a medical
& you show me friendship

come on let's skate!
anything can happen

Loughmore
John Liddy, 1963

More accustomed to bottoming
down on cardboard sleighs,
we abandoned the hill crest
for a Dutch scene in our Sunday best.

The thrill of knowing water lurked
beneath us, we glided across
towards the centre's solidity,
our hands raised triumphantly.

That summer we swam
in the current where we had skated
and believed in the miracle,
felt invincible.

Now when I look at the photograph
of the frozen lake that held my life,
I know the mirror does not reveal
what lies between the detail.

The Other Side of Winter
John McCullough
From The Frost Fairs (Salt, 2011)

Overnight the Thames begins to move again.
The ice beneath the frost fair cracks. Tents,
merry-go-rounds and bookstalls glide about

on islands given up for lost. They race,
switch places, touch – the printing press nuzzling
the swings – then part, slip quietly under.

Still, there is no end of crystal weather.
I hoard coal, stare mostly at the chimney's back,
fingering the pipe he gave me on the quay.

Even now it carries his greatcoat's whiff:
ale, oranges, resolve. I remember his prison-ship
lurking out from shore, huge as Australia.

I'll write, my dear sweet man, he said
then squeezed my thigh and turned, a sergeant
again, bellowing at a flock of convicts.

I do not have the nerve to light it.
The mouthpiece is covered with teeth marks, sweat.
I look out at my museum-garden,

the shrubs locked in glass cases,
the latticework a galaxy of frozen dew.
There is no snow in New South Wales.

I cannot put the pipe down. It makes things happen.
Last week I heard a crash and ran outside to find
a jackdaw flat on the lawn. It must have fallen

from the sky, its wings fused together
by hardened sleet, its neck twisted as though broken
from straining to see the incredible.

Perfect Six
Susan Richardson

On the ice rink of my mind
is a spotlit skater,
dress as flimsy

as success, hair strained
back, wide smile a gash
that won't heal.

I'd expected, at most,
a three-minute free programme,
but whenever I close my eyes,

she's repeating her routine.
First she spins, never strays –
legs purée the air like blades

in a blender – then, speeding
backwards, leaps
into the slippery arms of space.

She craves a soundtrack
of applause, bouquets
of praise in cellophane,

a rink-size gold.
And she relies on no-one
to help her win them –

chips of scorn fly
from her skate tips
at Torvill for needing Dean.

I, though, want to melt
the ice, scatter the salt
of imperfection, turn up the heat

with disorderly thoughts.
I want the soles of both her feet
to meet a matte surface.

I want her soaring fear
of five-point-nine to
                              fall.

From 'Winter': A Poem
by James Thomson, 1726

                        Where the Rhine
Branch'd out in many a long canal extends,
From every province swarming, void of care,
Batavia rushes forth: and as they sweep
On sounding skates a thousand different ways,
In circling poise, swift as the winds along,
The then gay land is maddened all to joy.

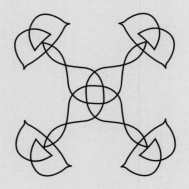

Acknowledgements

The poems 'Scating: A Poem' by Joseph Addison (1730), from 'Winter' a poem by James Thomson (1726), 'The Skaiter's March' by C. Dibdin (1802), 'Versus Ynne Praise of Scating' by Edgar Wood Syers (1904), 'An Elfin Skate' by Eugene Lee-Hamilton and 'Skating' by Robert Snow (1892) appeared in the anthology The Poetry of Skating by Edgar Wood Syers, published by Watts & Co., 1905.

Thanks to all who contributed to this festive collection of history and poetry. We could not have compiled such a wonderful collection without the help of Somerset House, the Museum of London, Jayne Torvill, Holly McConnell, Karen Smith, The Courtauld Institute of Art, Bert van Voorbergen (The Virtual Ice Skates Museum www.iceskatesmuseum.com), and all poets whose work has been included here.

At the Museum of London you can journey to the heart of London's story and discover the hidden treasures in the capital's history from 450,000 BC to the present day.

FREE Open daily 10am – 6pm. Closed 24-26 December. 150 London Wall, EC2Y 5HN

www.museumoflondon.org.uk

John McCullough's poem appears in The Frost Fairs (Salt, 2011)

And finally, Nigel Brown's, Ice-Skating: A History (Nicholas Kaye Ltd, 1959) proved to be an invaluable resource for the brief history of ice skating.

Profiles

Pauline Suett Barbieri is a Liverpool Poet shortlisted for the Bridport Poetry Prize by Sir Andrew Motion and twice for the Exeter Poetry Prize, by Jo Shapcott and Lawrence Sail respectively. An ancestor Richard 'Dicky' Suett (1755-1805) was George III's favourite Shakespearean clown and a star at Drury Lane for 25 years. Two collections out from Waterloo Press, Hove – The Shirley Valentine Syndrome (2002) and Bringing Home the Bacon (2012). The second inspired by the life and work of Francis Bacon (1909-1992).

Brendan Cleary is very widely published over the last 25 years. His most recent collection is 'Goin' Down Slow' Selected Poems (Tall Lighthouse, 2010).

Meredith Collins is an Assistant Editor at Pighog Press and is currently studying for a Masters in Creative and Critical writing at the University of Sussex. She has been published in a number of poetry anthologies and literary journals in the US and UK.

Tracy Davidson lives near Stratford-on-Avon, Warwickshire, and enjoys writing poetry and flash fiction. Her work has appeared in various publications and anthologies including: Mslexia, Roundyhouse, The Right-Eyed Deer, Atlas Poetica, Modern Haiku, Simply Haiku, A Hundred Gourds and Notes from the Gean. Apart from writing, Tracy enjoys reading thrillers and crime novels, photography, travel and walking the dog.

Anna Kisby's poems have been placed in competitions and published in magazines including Magma, Mslexia, The Interpreter's House, The Moth, Poetry News, 3AM and the Live Canon 2012 anthology. She was winner of the New Writer single poem prize 2011. She lives in Brighton and works as an archivist.

John Liddy was born in Youghal, Co Cork (1954), grew up in Limerick, took a degree in the University of Wales, works as a teacher in Madrid. His poetry books include Boundaries (1974); The Angling Cot (1991); Song of the Empty Cage(1997); Wine and Hope (1999); Cast-A-Net (2003); The Well: New and Selected Poems (2007); Gleanings from the Margins (2010). A new collection, Some Light Reading, due soon from Lapwing

Publications, Belfast, Ireland. He is the founding editor along with Jim Burke of The Stony Thursday Book, one of Ireland's longest running literary reviews along with Cyphers and organizes The Well/El Manantial, a weekend festival of poetry in Madrid with Matthew Loughney of The James Joyce Pub and The Embassy of Ireland.

John McCullough's first collection of poems The Frost Fairs (Salt, 2011) was a summer read in The Observer and was named a Book of the Year by The Independent and The Poetry School. The Guardian described it as 'sharp yet compassionate, formal yet nimble'. He teaches creative writing at Sussex University and the Open University and lives in Hove.

Susan Richardson is a poet, performer and educator based in Wales. Her most recent poetry collection, Where the Air is Rarefied (Cinnamon Press, 2011), is a collaboration with a printmaker on a range of environmental and mythological themes relating to the Far North. Susan regularly performs her work at festivals and other events throughout the UK and has been one of the resident poets of BBC Radio 4's Saturday Live. She has also been poet-in-residence for BBC 2's coverage of the Chelsea Flower Show and was recently invited to become a Fellow of the International League of Conservation Writers. For further information, please see *susanrichardsonwriter.co.uk*

Curtis Tappenden has been working as an author/illustrator for 25 years and has written 22 books on art & design practice. He also works as an editorial artist for The Mail on Sunday newspaper in London, and occasionally contributes travel writing for them as well. With a passion for performance Curtis tours shows around the country with his own inimitable and humorous brand of poetry with live painting. A qualified teacher, he lectures in Further Education and Creative Writing at the University for the Creative Arts in Kent & Surrey and is delighted to be included in this publication as a former artistic rolller dance skater for Great Britain. He lives with his wife, son and daughter on the South Coast in Brighton.

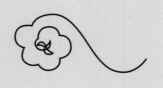